1971

ANTHROPOLOGY AND RELIGION

ANTHROPOLOGY
AND
RELIGION

BY

PETER HENRY BUCK
(TE RANGI HIROA)

PROFESSOR OF ANTHROPOLOGY, YALE UNIVERSITY
DIRECTOR OF THE BERNICE P. BISHOP MUSEUM
HONOLULU

ARCHON BOOKS
1970

ISBN: 0-208-00950-7
Library of Congress Catalog Card Number: 72-121753
Printed in the United States of America

CONTENTS

INTRODUCTION

THE Terry Lectures at Yale University deal with "Religion in the light of Science and Philosophy." They have been delivered by philosophers and eminent authorities in various branches of science but now, for the first time, the subject is approached by a humble anthropologist from the angle of a primitive religion.

Anthropology is a very wide subject, and even primitive religion is too extensive to be exhaustively discussed in three lectures. I will not pursue the academic method followed by Sir James Fraser in his *Golden Bough* whereby certain elements were isolated from the complex settings of which they formed an integral part. I prefer to follow the procedure of Professor Jung who, in his Terry Lectures on *Psychology and Religion*, confined himself to that part of psychology with which he was concerned in his medical practice. I will confine myself to the one ethnographical area with which I am best acquainted by reason of field work, namely, Polynesia.

Polynesia is an excellent field for study because, owing to its comparatively late settlement, we are enabled to obtain from the traditional records of its people a picture of the growth, elaboration, and decay of various social institutions which include religion. I will endeavor in this study of a primitive religion to apply the simple methods that are used in the study of a complex material structure, such as a house. I will commence on the ground with the erection of ridgeposts and wall posts, the subsequent addition of the upper framework and, last of all, the roof and walls which conceal the inner details. By starting from the ground, we may avoid the confusion of beginning in the clouds of metaphysics and philosophy. From the simple treatment of recorded material we may better appreciate the process of evolution that has taken place in religious concepts as well as in material things and social institutions. The book will therefore deal with the birth, growth, and decay of Polynesian religion under the following headings:

I.   Man Creates His Gods.
II.   The Gods Create Man.
III.   The Death of the Gods.

I

MAN CREATES HIS GODS

Polynesian Social Pattern

THE religion of the Polynesians was interwoven with a culture pattern that was developed in an oceanic environment. To understand the origin of the spiritual gods, it is necessary to discuss the origin of temporal leaders. The Polynesian voyages across the Pacific Ocean eastwards toward the rising sun were made in voyaging ships commanded by chiefs who exercised authority over crews composed of blood kinsmen and family retainers. The chiefs were advised by skilled navigators who by empirical study were enabled to interpret the natural phenomena that had a bearing on navigation. The appearance and movements of the heavenly bodies were studied as guides to season and direction. The annual lunar cycle had been established, and the seasons of the westerly winds and the southeast trades had been recorded in their minds. The months of the hurricane season were known, and the time for voluntary search expeditions for new lands were planned accordingly.

The chiefs inherited their rank and authority in

direct succession by primogeniture in the male line.
When a voyaging ship landed on an unoccupied island and permanent occupation was decided upon,
the chief as leader of his group superintended the
scheme of settlement. He decided where his head-
quarters should be located on the land in relation to
fresh water, fertile soil, and scenic attraction. He
divided the land among family heads and, when the
party was large, he established lesser chiefs to command districts which were given place names and def-
inite boundaries. The people looked to him for guidance, and their faith was justified. Hereditary chiefs
were born to leadership and they exercised their authority with wisdom.

The natural resources of the new land were ex-
plored for raw material in stone, wood, textile plants,
and native foods on land and sea. The food plants
that had been carried along in the voyaging canoes
were planted and cultivated. These were the coconut,
breadfruit, banana, plantain, arrowroot, *taro*, sweet
potato, and yam. The introduced domestic animals,
the pig, the dog, and the fowl were bred to increase
the food supplies of the new land.

As the population increased, the people formed an
extended family group claiming descent from common ancestors in the original family. The blood
kinship was further strengthened by marriages ar-

ranged to cement the blood tie. The extended family sought a name which would include all its members, and hence they had recourse to a distinguished ancestor from whom all were descended. A prefix, such as Ati or Ngati, was used before the proper name, and thus the descendants of Awa or Tane became the tribes of Ati-awa or Ngati-tane. The tribal system of blood descent and naming after an eponymous ancestor was widely spread in Polynesia, but in some areas, such as Hawaii and Samoa, groupings were based more on district occupation. In the tribal system, the eponymous ancestor received high honor in legend, song, and story, and his various deeds and exploits were the emotional inheritance of his descendants grouped together under his name.

As the descent group grew in size through the natural increase of succeeding generations, the number became too great to dwell close together in one locality. Family groups budded off from the main body and sought cultivable lands in fertile valleys farther away from the original focus. These groups were led by their own chiefs who were automatically established from the senior family in the migrating group. In the course of time, the secondary groups also grew in size and, in their turn, selected an eponymous ancestor from whom the particular sub-group was descended. Hence the original group had developed into a numerous tribe which the need for expansion into cultivable land had split up into a number of subtribes, each with its own name, territory, and ruling chiefs.

Although the newly developed subtribes occupied adjoining territory, the immediate family group of the original leader usually lived on in the first focus of settlement. Tradition and sentiment grew up about the earlier places of settlement, and a richer heritage of history was associated with the senior family in the tribe. Owing to the division of the tribe into subtribes, the family group remaining in the original settlement may be regarded also as a subtribe, but it was senior in precedence to the others. In many instances, this senior subtribe did not give itself a new subtribal name but merely retained its original designation which had become a tribal name. It was the people who moved out that required new names.

The senior line of descent from the original leader supplied chiefs who were senior in rank and prestige to the subtribal chiefs. They were chief of chiefs and received the special title of *ariki*. The subtribes had budded off from the senior family after the establishment of the senior chieftainship, and hence the titles of their chiefs were more recent in time as well as junior in birth. Each subtribe was a separate unit tracing descent to its own eponymous ancestor of more recent date, but all the subtribes could trace their lineage back to the earlier ancestor who gave his name to the tribe. Each subtribe managed its own local affairs under the direction of its own chiefs, but questions of policy that affected the tribe as a whole were decided at gatherings of the subtribal chiefs meeting in conference with the tribal chief or *ariki*.

In tropical Polynesia, where fertile land was not so extensive as in New Zealand, the land was portioned out to meet the needs of the people. Theoretically the title to land rested with the chiefs whose ancestors had been given original grants. The chiefs apportioned their lands to the heads of families in their groups and were paid rent in the form of a share of the produce from the cultivations, fowls, and pigs raised on the land and manufactured goods, such as bark cloth. Fishermen brought choice fish to their chiefs. The lesser chiefs, in their turn, rendered food and goods to the tribal chief as acknowledgment of the fact that they had received their charter to the land from the original leader. In some islands, the chiefs rendered fealty to the high chief by rethatching his house when repairs were needed.

They supported him by providing food and goods on the marriage of his daughter and on such special occasions as he might command.

With a growing population and an increasing social development, individuals acquired expert knowledge in fishing, horticulture, building canoes and houses, war, and the various activities that made up the culture of the people. They became specialists and leaders in the local development of the arts and crafts.

In the general evolution that took place with an increasing population, social accretions grew up around the chiefs and, particularly, the senior or high chief. The position of the high chief was invested with those typical Polynesian attributes, *mana* and *tapu* (taboo). The *mana*, which means power and prestige, was derived from senior descent in the male line, and the increasing power of a growing tribe was symbolized in the person of the high chief. The *tapu* or sanctity of his person was also derived from his high descent and the awe and respect that accompanies increasing power. The *mana* and *tapu* of a high chief were not only hereditary but were increased by the allegiance and support of a powerful tribe. The status of the chief was enhanced by religious observances carried out at his birth, installation, and various social occasions during his life and in the funeral ceremonies following his death. In Tahiti such observances were marked by human sacrifice. After death, the spirits of chiefs and commoners passed on to the spirit land, a mysterious region situated toward the setting sun, where the cradle of the race was to be found. Sometimes they returned in dreams and hallucinations, and so was sown the seed that grew into the belief in immortality.

The Creation of Gods

Religion has been defined as a system of faith and worship. The Polynesians had supreme faith in their chiefs and they reverenced them to the point of worship. In Tonga, when people entered the house of the sacred Tui-tonga chief, they knelt before him and touched the soles of his feet with the backs of their hands, sometimes with their forehead. In offering this sign of respect, the very act of touching imbued them with some of the sacred chief's taboo. They repeated the act on leaving his presence and thus returned the taboo. If the chief were engaged in conversation at the time of leaving, they touched a small wooden bowl placed outside the door for the purpose. It was believed that if the act of returning the taboo were not done, the person became ill. In Tahiti, people stripped to the waist as the high chief went by. He was carried on the shoulders of bearers, because, if he walked, the land touched by his feet became impregnated with his taboo and so could not be used by others. In Hawaii, people sat down or prostrated themselves on the ground according to the rank of the chief. These observances approached worship but they were made to living men. The chief came near to divinity but he was not a god.

The definition of religion quoted above is incomplete but it is rounded off by adding that religion includes the recognition of a superhuman controlling power. Any superhuman controlling power must come from beyond man himself. Man may act as a medium but a living man cannot be a god. To become a god, man must pass through the portals of death. Death may be the end of material life, but it is the beginning of a spiritual immortality.

The Polynesian leaders had full confidence in their ability to deal with mundane affairs but they recognized that there were some things beyond human power. Such were control of the elements, fertility of food plants, movements of fish, and assured success in war and other undertakings. Western civilization in comparatively recent times has solved many problems by means of applied science. In stone-age Polynesia, science remained empirical, and the Polynesians followed the ancient urge of seeking aid from some supernatural controlling power.

The Christian concept of immortality is essentially selfish. The soul of the person who has acquired merit in this world passes on to its reward in another world and remains there. Shakespeare speaks of "The free and undiscovered country from whose bourne no traveller returns." The gates of death are shut and there is no possible return of the spirit. In the Polynesian concept, however, the gates remain open and the spirits of those who have passed on may return to this world. Their return was sometimes inconvenient. In order to establish some link with the supernatural, it seems natural that the Polynesians should have recalled the spirits of certain of their illustrious ancestors to establish control over problems that were beyond the power of man. They had solved problems during their sojourn in this life and why should they not continue to exercise a supernatural power in the life beyond? The spirits recalled for aid were selected by man, and so the Polynesians created their gods.

Deification

The first process involved in building up Polynesian religion was the deification of ancestors. All ancestors who figure in the lineages were respected by their descendants but they were not all worshiped. Only those that had been selected were deified as gods. The method of deification was simple. A member of a family, not necessarily the chief but a person who was psychic, established communication with the ancestral spirit by means of invocations and offerings. He became the medium of the spirit and, when consultations were desired, the spirit took possession or entered the body of the medium and used the medium's voice to announce his presence.

Spiritualism

I see little difference between this beginning and the spiritualistic séances that are still conducted in Western society. There is a vast difference however in subsequent development. In the civilized séances, the spirit remains a vague unit with nothing to communicate for the good of society, and the medium remains an individual who is treated with suspicion and disbelief by the great majority, who do not believe in spiritualism. The development in uncivilized society reached a loftier plane. The spirit became a god who conferred benefits upon his worshipers, and the medium became a priest of high standing.

Sorcery

Two fields existed in which the return of the spirits from the other world was not for the public good. Just as in this world there were good and evil persons, so in the other world there were good and evil spirits. An evil-minded person conjured back an evil spirit to slay his enemies or the enemies of those who had paid him. The evil spirit became the familiar spirit of the person whose commands it obeyed and that person went into practice as a sorcerer. The familiar spirits were not worshiped as gods by the family or the people, and the sorcerer was both despised and feared. In Western society, of course, witches and sorcerers who were supposed to have a contract with the devil were believed in until recent times.

Disease Demons

The other field in which spirits were evil was that of sickness and disease. Just as the sorcerer sent his familiar spirit to attack the vitals of a victim, so the abnormal symptoms that marked a departure from normal health were believed to be caused by disease demons that were evil spirits from the other world. These disease demons were held to be derived from the spirits of those who had never reached maturity in this world: abortions and miscarriages. It would seem that such spirits, having been frustrated in this life by not reaching maturity, sought revenge on human beings by entering their bodies and bringing about the abnormal symptoms that are caused by disease. But even here there had to be some reason for the attack, and the reason generally given was an infringement by the patient of one of the many taboos. The established pattern was that particular disease demons belonged to the family in which the abortion or miscarriage had occurred, and it was the infringement of the taboos of that family that the disease demon punished. The treatment consisted in identifying the disease demon that was present in the patient and then asking the leading member of the family owning the demon to remove it. The removal or casting out of the evil spirit was accomplished by exorcism, the recital of a command, or some ritual phrases. In civilized society, we have an example of exorcism where Christ cast out the evil spirits from a sick man. The evil spirits entered the bodies of swine which dashed over a cliff and so destroyed themselves. The Polynesians could not afford to waste their limited quantity of swine so, during the exorcism, a material object of no economic value, such as a reed or toy canoe, was provided; and, after the disease demon had entered this form of transport, it was floated away on a stream or the ocean back to the unknown. From its wide distribution in Polynesia, this simple form of bedside treatment seems to have been the earlier pattern, but later some of the disease demons were raised to the status of minor gods controlling disease by mediums, who, by a more elaborate ritual, raised their own status to that of minor priests. The elevation of disease demons into minor gods is well exemplified in the religion of Mangareva.*

Gods

After this diversion, let us return to the real gods. The deified ancestors that were recalled by a psychic medium to assist the family in its earthly struggles became a family god, worshiped by all members of the family, and the family medium became the family priest. As the family expanded into a tribe, the god increased in influence to become a tribal god. If the tribe extended its influence by conquering neighboring tribes and absorbing the conquered, the prestige or *mana* of the god increased with the temporal power of its worshipers. Hence by a process of evolution, a god commencing as a family god could rise with its increasing number of worshipers into a tribal god and ultimately into a major god, worshiped over an island or an island group. The spiritual power of a god depended on the temporal power of its worshipers, consolidated and retained by success in war.

Polytheism

The Polynesians, however, were not content with one god, for the system of religion was influenced by

* P. H. Buck (Te Rangi Hiroa), "Ethnology of Mangareva," *Bishop Museum Bulletin* 157 (Honolulu, 1938).

the native culture of the people. In the struggle for existence, they recognized that it was impossible for one person to be expert in all avenues of life. Hence experts arose in different vocations, such as fishing, horticulture, war, and the various arts and crafts. They studied the sun, moon, stars, winds, and natural phenomena that had a bearing on planting, fishing, and sea voyages. It is natural then that they should have created a god to preside over the various departments of life as they saw them. Hence Polynesian religion was polytheistic. A Polynesian once informed an early missionary that he could not understand how one god could possibly attend to all the varied demands made upon him. In his religion, a person consulted the god of his particular need and had more chance of receiving attention. Hence he considered that the Polynesian religion was superior to Christianity.

The Priesthood

The family medium, with the increase in power of his god and of his people, also shared the growth in importance. He became a tribal priest, and, when his god became a national or major god, he became a high priest with exceedingly great power. The position, like other social positions, became hereditary in the male line. He inherited not merely the

position but he learned and transmitted the correct
ritual and observances that developed through successive generations. He became a scholar versed in
the mythology of his culture, and he was responsible
for making additions to the expanding theology. He
built up taboos around his god and around himself.
He made known the requirements of his god to the
people through direct possession or by interpreting
various omens that were manifestations of the divine
will.

The Temple

Having established a god, it was necessary to set
aside some place where the correct observances could
be carried out in an appropriate manner. For a family god a simple shrine consisting of an erected stone
or post was quite sufficient. The stone or post marked
a locality which was imbued with taboo. These simple shrines are present in various islands, and in
New Zealand this simple form was retained as the
general pattern.

In central, northern, and eastern Polynesia, the
tribal and national gods were worshiped on more
complex structures. The simple stone upright developed into a raised stone platform, and a paved
court was made before it for the accommodation of
a multiple priesthood and chiefly worshipers. The

raised platform was termed *ahu,* and the court was
the *marae.* Social as well as religious functions were
conducted on the open court, and elaboration in
structure took various forms in different island
groups. In New Zealand, a divorce took place between the *ahu* altar and the *marae* court. Religious
observances took place at the *ahu* shrine outside the
village, and social gatherings took place on the open
space before the village guest house. This social
court retained the name of *marae.*

In the west in Samoa and Tonga, the temple took
the form of a house on a raised platform made on
the same plan as a dwelling house. It was surrounded
by a fence, and both the building and the enclosed
space were taboo.

Material Representatives

It would appear that the Polynesians, having created unseen spiritual gods, followed a human need
in desiring some material objects to represent them.
Here again, there was great variation in the objects
selected. In Samoa and Tonga, simple objects, such
as stones, whales' teeth, a bowl, or a weapon were
used to represent the god. They were wrapped in
bark cloth and kept in a basket in the religious structure and only exposed by the priest to worshipers
when they needed the god's assistance. In other re-

gions, images were made in wood and stone. Some very large images in stone were made in the Marquesas, Austral Islands, and Easter Island. These were set up in the open temples as permanent fixtures and, as such, it is doubtful whether they were regarded as gods or ornaments. The smaller images that represented gods were wrapped up in bark cloth and kept in charge of the priests. They were treated with reverence and exposed to the public eye only during temple ceremonies. The carving of images was purely conventional and differed markedly in the different island groups. There was no attempt to follow closely the anatomical proportions of the human body.

In central Polynesia, an increasing importance was attached to red feathers as a symbol of the divine. In the Society Islands, images in human form were abandoned as symbols of the gods, and they were taken up by sorcerers as habitats for their familiar spirits. The priests adopted a new technique by covering cylindrical pieces of wood with a fine twine in coconut-husk fiber. Eyes, nose, mouth, hands, and the navel were depicted by pieces of sennit cord attached to the twined work. Beautiful red feathers of the native parakeet tied to sennit carriers were attached to the front surface of the covered cylinder. Some of these gods had the wood exposed at the

ends, and there was no attempt to add human features. In all, however, the presence of red feathers
was essential. They were first consecrated by the high
priest, who kept them for a period with the temple
image of the district god. In the Cook Islands,
wooden images were made in Rarotonga and Aitutaki, but carved wooden stands with small arches for
the attachment of feathers were used in the other
islands of the group. Not all gods were materially
represented. It would appear that the older gods,
who had become classical and academic and were no
longer invoked for creature benefits, were not represented symbolically in wood or stone. The material
symbols were for those gods that were invoked for
material assistance. All these various forms were inanimate symbols of the gods, and though regarded
as taboo, they were not worshiped in themselves.
Hence the term idolatry applied to Polynesian religion by rival theologians is not quite accurate.

Animate Representatives

The inanimate symbols of the divinity could give
no movement or sign to indicate his will to his followers. Man down the ages has seen omens and por-
tents in the movements and action of birds and living
things. The Polynesians shared this attitude and in-
stitutionalized matters by associating the various

gods with particular birds or animals. These animals
were regarded as incarnations of the gods, for the
gods manifested themselves through them. In Mangaia, the god Tane was incarnate in a black bird
named *mo'o* (*moho*), and when a follower of Tane
was being treacherously guided into an ambush, a
mo'o bird flew across his path making a scolding
noise. This was the god Tane warning his follower
not to go on. Various birds, fish, and lizards have
been chosen as incarnations. There is generally a
story or myth creating some connection between the
deified ancestor and the animal that became incarnate. The deified ancestor Te A'ia of Mangaia was
killed in a stream, and his blood was swallowed by an
eel. Hence the eel became the incarnation of the god
Te A'ia. The eel went out to sea and was swallowed
by a shark. Hence the shark also became an incarnation of Te A'ia. Although individual worshipers
could interpret some of the signs made by the incarnate animal, it was the priests who were the official interpreters and who established the particular
meanings of the omens.

Offerings

The temporal chief was given presents of food
and material goods as a mark of respect and, in like
manner, offerings of food or some material object

were made to the gods. The gods got their share
and through such recognition they were amicably
disposed toward their followers. One marked difference existed between the temporal presents and the
religious offerings. Since the chiefs ate the food and
used the goods, quantity was desirable. The offerings
to the gods were purely symbolical, and the act of
offering something was all that was needed to insure
the favor of the gods. Hence a fisherman on his way
to sea placed a coral pebble or a stone on the shrine
of a tutelary deity of fish to promote a good catch.
On his return, he might place a fish on the shrine as
a mark of his gratitude. He shared his catch with
his god as well as with his chief or neighbor, and the
religious offering followed the pattern of social sharing of food when the occasion warranted. The unsuccessful fisherman placed a stone on the shrine on
his return in the hope of better luck next time. In the
atolls where vegetable foods were limited, the coconut was all important. The symbolic nature of the
offering is exemplified in Tongareva, where a piece
of coconut husk was the orthodox offering during
the temple ritual. In Mangaia, there was a keeper of
the tribal gods that were kept in a god house under
his care. Every evening he fed each of the dozen gods
with *taro* cooked in a fire used only for that purpose. The fire was small and only one tuber was

heated on the embers. The keeper broke off a small piece of the tuber and, holding it aloft in his hand toward the god house, he addressed one of the gods by name, saying, "O Motoro, here is your food. Eat!" He then threw the piece of *taro* into the bushes near the house. So, in turn, he fed all the gods with the one small *taro*. It was of no consequence that the *taro* was not properly cooked and the portions were small. The gods absorbed the spiritual essence of the food, and it was the symbolic action that satisfied them. In Mangareva, when the people cooked their meals, a small portion was set aside for the gods on a stone table before the family god house. A daily offering was made also in the atolls of Manihiki and Rakahanga but, in most islands, the offerings were made when the god was invoked for a specific purpose or on special occasions, such as the completion of a temple, the gathering of first fruits, the opening of fishing or hunting seasons, and the services that took place in the temples from time to time. In New Zealand, the first fish caught on a closed fishing ground was put back into the sea as an offering to the local god of fish or was taken ashore to hang on a tree or rock that formed the shrine of the deity. Similarly the first pigeon caught on the opening of the season was cast aside into the bushes with a ritual phrase as an offering to the god of the forests. The first fish or bird having been offered to the gods, the people were at liberty to take as many as they could catch. When the Tahitian canoe builders killed a pig ceremonially before they engaged in building an important craft, the first tuft of hair removed in cleaning the pig was held aloft and offered to Tane, the god of canoe builders. When the pig was cooked, the tail was offered to Tane. It may seem that the selection of the parts offered to the god was influenced by economic reasons, and religious zeal did not obscure common sense. The gods enjoyed the spiritual symbol, and the builders enjoyed the material pork.

In the fertile soil of the Society Islands in central Polynesia, where both cultivable foods and animal food in the form of pork were abundant, the food offerings to the gods also became greater not only in variety but in quantity. We have seen that when the canoe builders of that area made their offerings to their tutelary god, they retained the simple pattern of older times. In the great celebrations on the national temples, however, ritual elaboration took place to a marked degree. This was primarily due to the growth of a powerful hereditary priesthood, who interpreted the wants of the gods in terms of their own human desires. The temple celebrations, like all social gatherings of importance, were marked by the accumulation of large quantities of vegetables, fruit, fish, and pork to provide a feast for the congregation. The food, according to Polynesian custom, was divided into shares for the chiefs and family groups and, as the gathering was of a religious nature, a fitting share had to be set aside for the gods. On such occasions the gods, as represented by a numerous priesthood and their attendants, were no longer satisfied with the symbolism of a morsel of *taro* or a tuft of pig's hair. As interpreted by the priests, the gods required both quantity and quality. Hence the best vegetables, fruits, fish, and fattened pigs were brought in by the various family groups as their offerings to the gods. The priests took charge of the offerings and, with an elaborate ritual, presented them to the gods. The food was rendered taboo and could not be eaten by anyone outside of the priesthood. The gods, having partaken of the spiritual essence of the offerings, the food itself was eaten by the priests and their attendants on the temple courtyard. The congregation on the outside of the temple were then at liberty to feast on the secular food that had been allotted to them. Thus, just as man created god in his own image, so an organized priesthood interpreted him in terms of their own human needs.

Human Offerings

It is apparent from the history of various island groups that the Polynesians, like other early peoples, believed in sympathetic magic. As an offering of the first fruits would insure or increase the fertility of crops, so an offering of a person killed in war would promote success in future military campaigns. In New Zealand, where stress was laid on the first object killed or secured, as in the first fish or the first bird, so in war importance was laid on the first person killed in battle. The New Zealanders seem to have adhered to an early pattern of offering a part of the victim on the spot where the first person fell. There was no time to wait for a more elaborate ritual on temple ground. The priest of the party that slew the first man in battle immediately removed the victim's heart and held it aloft as an offering to the war god of his tribe. He also cut off a lock of hair, which was placed on the tribal shrine when the war party returned home. The first slain in battle was termed the "first fish" (*mata-ika*), which indicates that to a seafaring people the memory remains of fish being an early form of offering to the gods.

In Mangaia, the body of an enemy slain in battle was offered on the temple of the victors. In the growth of ritual that took place, a victim was selected from a conquered tribe and killed as a special offering for the temple installation of the leader of the victorious forces who became dictator over the island. The human offering was also termed the "fish" (*ika*). It was held that the human offering to the god Rongo would insure a peaceful rule with plenteous seasons of food. The offering was not eaten but was cast into the bushes behind the temple as food for Papa, who was paradoxically the mother of the gods.

Human offerings were common on the other island groups except on some of the atolls and in the west. Where cannibalism prevailed, they were eaten by the priests. In the Society Islands, where the eating of human flesh was not indulged in, a form of symbolic eating took place. The high priest handed an eye of the victim to the high chief, who passed it across his mouth and returned it to the priest. A human offering was the greatest of all offerings and was used only on important occasions. There is no doubt that at times the system was abused by chiefs and priests who indicated as an offering some person they wanted to have removed. On the other hand, in some ceremonies in the Society Islands a young banana plant was substituted for the human offering and was referred to as the "long banana man." The human offering was also termed a "fish." Hence it is evident that, just as the young banana plant could on occasion be substituted for a human being, so the human being was originally a substitute for an offering of fish. The plant retained the term "man," and man retained the term "fish."

I have referred throughout to the human victim as an offering rather than a sacrifice. A sacrifice should involve a certain amount of acquiescence on the part of the person who formed the offering. The persons offered were unwilling victims of the despotism of chiefs and priests. When families from whom victims were likely to be selected learned of an impending ceremony that demanded a human offering, they hid themselves in the mountains and forests until the ceremony was over. Instances occurred in Mangaia, however, in which chiefs and priests offered themselves voluntarily as human sacrifices in order that the tribes to which they belonged might attain victory in an impending war. The sacrifice was made known to their tribal priests in order that they might make the spiritual offering to the gods. The self-appointed victim then exposed himself to death at the hands of the enemy. The killing completed the sacrifice and insured victory in the minds of the tribe for whom the sacrifice was made. Greater love hath no man than this, that he give up his life for his tribe.

Temple Furnishings

With the growth of religious ritual, houses were built on the hitherto open court to accommodate the priests and their assistants during the temple ceremonies. It must be remembered, however, that the temples were not in constant use. Early European explorers, who wrote about the neglected state of some of the temples, saw them at a time when they were not being used for an actual ceremony. In the tropics, plants grow very quickly, of course, and the atmosphere of permanent disuse is deceptive. Before an important ceremony, the people were assembled by the priests, and the temple courtyard and surroundings were cleared and weeded. Any necessary repairs to the stonework and woodwork upon the court were made by the priests and their attendants.

In addition to the house or houses for accommodation, a sacred house was provided for the images or other material representatives of the gods. In the Society Islands, a wooden litter was provided for the national god, and during the ceremony the litter was carried by special attendants and placed on a low stone pavement in front of the large stone platform of the temple. Drums used during the ceremony were also kept on the court together with other temple regalia, such as the costumes of the priests. The in-

creased quantity of the offerings necessitated the
building of raised wooden platforms to support the
pigs and other offerings to be made to the gods and
subsequently eaten by the priests.

In some temples stone pillars were erected on various parts of the temple. In the Society Islands,
carved wooden slabs were placed upright in various
parts for ornamentation. In Hawaii, an oracle tower
in three tiers was built on the court and covered with
bark cloth. Large wooden temple images were erected
on the court in Hawaii, and large images of stone
were similarly displayed in the Marquesas, Austral
Islands, and Easter Island. Hence in the various
groups, the place where religious ritual was conducted varied from a simple stone shrine to an open
paved temple with various furnishings.

Ritual

The ritual employed shared in the general growth
and varied from simple phrases used by individuals
to the intoned chants and invocations led by high
priests in solo parts and joined in chorus by the body
of lesser priests. It is evident that successive generations of priests added their compositions to what had
been handed down to them orally. Words used in the
incantations have become archaic and, though the

meanings are sometimes difficult to translate, they were believed to be effective purely from their sound and use. There was a magic in words. It is exemplified in the New Zealand phrase to avert disaster:

> Kuruki, whakataha.
> Evil, pass by.

A longer example is provided by the incantation used by a Maori warrior in tying on his war belt before engaging in battle. Though no mention is made of a war god, the words describing the feelings of the warrior were in themselves supposed to bring about supernatural assistance.

> Homai taku maro,
> Kia hurua,
> Kia rawea,
> Kia harapaki maua ko te riri,
> Kia harapaki maua ko te nguha.
> He maro riri te maro,
> He maro nguha te maro,
> He maro kai taua.

> Give me my war belt,
> To be girded,
> To be fastened,

> That I may join with wrath,
> That I may unite with rage.
> The belt is a belt of wrath,
> The belt is a belt of rage,
> A belt that destroys armies.

These examples from New Zealand belong to an early phase that relied on supernatural assistance by the magic of words.

In other areas, such as Tahiti and Hawaii, the chants used were invocations that appealed directly to a specific god for military success, food, and the various needs of the worshipers. When words in themselves were regarded as magical, the correct rendering of the words of the incantation became obligatory. Any mistake in the words or their sequence in the chant was regarded as an ill omen for the reciting priest. Sooner or later, he met death in some form or other, and the death was attributed to punishment by the gods for a broken ritual.

Summary

To summarize this chapter I have tried to picture the growth of a primitive religion in one ethnological area. I have endeavored to relate the historical sequence of events from the simple to the complex. Man, realizing from dreams perhaps that there was a spiritual essence or soul that was not destroyed but merely freed from its material envelope, evolved the concept of immortality. The souls of the Polynesian ancestors lived on in the spirit land of Hawaiki. Their descendants called upon them for assistance in the problems of this life. They wished for a continuity of help and so deified specific ancestors as gods who could be consulted when occasion demanded. Thus man created his gods. The Polynesian created his gods in his own image because, after all, they had once been living persons with human desires and passions. They had had wives and begat children; they had had their loves and infidelities much like the gods on Mount Olympus. Like Jehovah, they were jealous gods, but they did not visit the sins of the fathers upon the children to the third and fourth generation. They were given the supernatural power that man desired but could not himself possess. With a belief in that power, man was inspired to accomplish many things that he might otherwise not have attempted. The religious beliefs of the Polynesians were founded on faith just as much as were the tenets of the better-known religions. By faith they were able to remove the mountains of doubt and fear. Faith in their gods supplemented by innate courage and supreme daring enabled them to cross the thou-

sands of leagues of the vast Pacific stretching between southeast Asia and South America and so to
complete the most marvelous Odyssey the world has
ever known.

II

THE GODS CREATE MAN

Introduction

A COMPARATIVE study of the details of the religion in the different island groups of Polynesia reveals the interesting fact that, while some of the names of the gods are common and shared, a large number of names are purely local and are not shared by other islands. The historical time sequence shows that the shared gods had their birth before dispersal took place from some common center, and that the local gods, many of whose names occur in the family lineages, originated after the particular island was settled. Some of the local gods are so recent that on the advent of Christianity they were family gods that had not reached the status of tribal gods. The older gods that were shared by so many islands we may consider as major gods, while those of more recent date and of purely local origin we may regard as minor gods. Let us seek the home of the major gods, where the foundations of Polynesian belief were laid.

Cultural Center of Polynesia

The Polynesian people inhabit the islands included in a vast triangle formed by Hawaii in the north, New Zealand in the south, and Easter Island in the east. The portal of entry of the early navigators is on the western base line stretching between Hawaii and New Zealand, and the apex is at Easter Island, the most easterly island of Polynesian settlement. The Society Islands form the geographical center of the triangle.

A comparative study of the myths, legends, traditions, genealogies, and historical narratives of Polynesia indicates convincingly that the cultural center corresponds with the geographical center, the Society Islands. From this center, eight radiating lines along the main cardinal points of the compass lead to the various island groups settled by the Polynesians. On all these radials, except the one to the west, the names of the major gods occur. The western radial leads to Samoa and Tonga, and in these groups the name of but one major god is known. From this distribution, it would appear that the descendants of the other major gods must have made their way direct from Micronesia to the Society Islands without passing through Samoa.

In the Society Islands, legend and tradition attribute seniority in chieftainship and in the priesthood to the island of Ra'iatea, of which the ancient name was Havai'i, the Hawaiki of New Zealand legends. On this island a powerful priesthood arose in the district of Opoa. Here a religious temple, beginning in a simple form, grew in size and importance until it became the great international temple of Taputapu-atea. I visited this temple in 1929. The walls of the raised platform were formed of limestone slabs that rose twelve feet above the ground. Some of these outer slabs had fallen to the ground and revealed the inner, lower slabs of an earlier structure. Thus the process of decay revealed the growth that had taken place in the past. In the heyday of its fame, chiefs and priests had sailed to this ancient religious center from the near-by island groups to lay their offerings on the sacred temple of Taputapu-atea.

The Major Gods

In order not to confuse the reader with unfamiliar names, I will submit but four of the major gods in this brief outline of Polynesian religion. These are Tane, Rongo, Tu, and Tangaroa, names which, I think, will not be found in Indonesia or the early lands from whence the Polynesians came. Knowing what happened in the development of selected ancestral names into names for social groups or tribes and in the deification of selected ancestors as gods, I feel that the Polynesian technique of deifying ancestors applies to the major gods I have mentioned. I believe that the major gods—Tane, Rongo, Tu, Tangaroa—and the other older gods were navigating ancestors who guided their voyaging ships through the later part of the eastward movement through Micronesia into the Society Islands. They may have actually landed on these islands, for Raʻiatea was peopled for some centuries before dispersal took place. There was ample time for them to be deified and then to become enshrouded with the mists of antiquity. The older ancestral gods that were worshiped in the land of origin or were created along the early part of the eastward voyages were dropped, forgotten, and supplanted by later deified ancestors.

It may be taken for granted that the various family groups that developed in Raʻiatea worshiped the particular deified ancestor from whom they were descended. They paid particular deference to their own deified ancestor but were well acquainted with the gods of their neighbors. We have historical evidence of this in the traditions that wars took place between the different major gods. The wars of the gods were the struggles that took place between the descendants of those who created them.

The Growth of Theology

As the temple of Taputapu-atea rose to fame, so did the prestige of the priests associated with it. The priests formed a religious seminary which combined the fragments of myths that had filtered through with the early voyagers and worked them into a pattern to form a theology that was influenced by their oceanic background. "The priests gathered together the warp of myth and the weft of history and wove them into the textile of theology." * The various major gods who had different family origins had their advocates among the priests. Claims to precedence were settled by bringing the major gods together in one family by making them the children of the same father and mother.

The priests, influenced by the social custom of sharing food and material goods, proceeded to share or divide supernatural influence and power among the family of gods. The original sharing of power is revealed to us by the patterns that persisted in the marginal groups of islands that are separated from the center by long expanses of ocean. They ad-

* P. H. Buck (Te Rangi Hiroa), *Vikings of the Sunrise* (New York, 1938).

hered to an early pattern and did not participate in the further development that occurred in the center after dispersal had taken place.

In this early form of supernatural government by the gods, special departments were created for the major gods. The major gods became departmental gods and were appealed to according to the particular desires of the people. Tane was given Forestry and hence controlled trees, birds, and insect life. He naturally became the tutelary deity of wood craftsmen. Before a tree could be felled in the forest for a voyaging ship or an important house, Tane had to be placated with a ritual chant or invocation; and before commencing an important task, an offering was made to Tane by the craftsmen. Tu was given the department of War, and warriors were dedicated to his service. Rongo presided over Horticulture and Food and, as a plentiful supply can be produced by cultivation only in a time of peace, Rongo also became God of Peace. Tangaroa ruled over the Marine Department and hence was appealed to by deep-sea voyagers and fishermen. This simple, straightforward pattern occurs in New Zealand, but, while the main principles also exist in other marginal groups, certain changes occur. Thus some gods are given greater influence and others are demoted.

The Parents of the Gods

Having created major gods, placed them in one family, and given them departments to rule over, the priests were faced with the problem of creating parents for them. Here they entered the realm of metaphysics. No ordinary living persons could be given the posts of parents of gods, so the priesthood personified natural phenomena to fill the positions. The male parent was Atea, the personification of space which lies above the surface of land and sea; the female parent was Papa, the personification of the earth stratum, or land. It is interesting here to theorize on the symbolism of the Sky-father and the Earth-mother. It seems natural that a seafaring people who voyaged over open spaces and wide expanses of ocean in search of land should personify space and earth. However, the concept of the Sky-father and the Earth-mother occurs back in Indonesia, whence the Polynesians came. The concept appears to be too old to have originated in Polynesia itself, and apparently it is one of the myths that was carried along from an ancient homeland. Though it occurs in various forms along seven radials, it is not present in the west. Granted a ready-made Sky-father and Earth-mother, what the priests at Opoa did was to cone newly created major gods to an older myth.

In some islands, two other mythical characters were associated with Atea and Papa. They were Te Tumu (Cause), a male, and Hakahotu (To-take-form), a female. In Penrhyn atoll, Atea married Hakahotu and produced the gods. In Rarotonga, Te Tumu married Papa and produced the gods. In Hawaii, Wakea (Atea) married both Papa and Ho'-ohoku (Hakahotu) and produced islands. In the revised mythology of Tahiti, Atea was first a female and then changed sexes with Fa'ahotu (Hakahotu) to become a male. It is evident that different schools in personifying the ideas of a primary cause and material form have mixed them up with the clear-cut concept of Atea and Papa, who gave birth to the gods.

Space having been personified as the Sky-father, some explanation had to be given of why he was so far removed from the Earth-mother. The Sky-father was termed Atea, Vatea, and Wakea in various islands. In the Marquesas, he had the double name of Atea-Rangi, and in New Zealand, the word Atea was dropped and Rangi retained, so that the Sky-father became Rangi (Sky). In order to carry out the theme of the primary parents giving birth to the gods, the human method of reproduction was followed. The Sky-father was materialized as a male who originally embraced the Earth-mother and remained in close touch with her. Their children—Tane, Rongo, Tu, Tangaroa, and others—were born and lay between them in a circumscribed world of darkness. In the New Zealand version, the children complained of darkness and lack of space. Some, led by Tane, determined to separate their parents in order to obtain light and space, but a conservative party, led by Whiro, opposed the plan. However, the iconoclasts prevailed, and Tane took the principal part in effecting the separation. At first he tried to push the Sky-parent upwards with his arms but failed. He then inverted himself and, standing on his head, pushed upwards with his feet. This form of leverage was more successful and so Rangi, the Sky-father, was separated from the Earth-mother and relegated to his present position. Trees, which are the children of Tane, are figuratively held to represent the position of Tane during this great feat. The roots represent the hair of the head, which is down in the ground, and the branches are the feet which pushed upwards.

In some island groups, Ru is credited with the task of pushing up the sky. In the Cook Islands, Ru was successful without any bodily ill effect. In Tahiti, however, he failed and contracted an inguinal hernia through the muscular strain. In Tuamotu, he bent

his spine and was termed Ru-the-humpback. Raising
the sky was a wonderful theme to which various details were added. In the tropical islands where arrowroot grew, the Sky was raised in stages. In the first,
low stage, it rested on the leaves of the arrowroot
which thus became permanently flattened. In New
Zealand, where there was no arrowroot, the arrowroot stage of elevation does not occur.

The Sky having been raised on high, light came
into their world and the gods were enabled to assume
the erect position. The god Tane attached the sun,
moon, and stars to the breast of the Sky-father, and
day was divided from night. The god Whiro, who
had led the opposition, retired into the underworld
to live in the darkness that he preferred.

The Era of Darkness

The organization of a theology did not stop at the
creation of the Sky-father and the Earth-mother and
the details connected with them. There was a vague
period preceding them, which began with Chaos and
Darkness. The literary tools used by the Polynesian mythologists were personification and genealogy.
Chaos or Void was personified by Kore (Nothing)
and the primeval darkness by Po (Night). In some
versions, the prolonged period of darkness was num-

bered as the First Night, the Second Night, and so on in sequence to the Tenth Night. In other versions, the Po received qualifying terms, such as Po-tinitini (Myriad Nights), Po-tangotango (Impenetrable Night), and Po-kerekere (Abysmal Night). Darkness was succeeded by various degrees of light from the merest flicker to perceptible light. In the classical Kumu-lipo chant of Hawaii, there are eleven eras of darkness, and the recital of each era ends with the sentence, "It is night." The twelfth era ends the long period of night, and the canto ends with the significant sentence, "It is light." Thus natural phenomena in varying degrees of intensity were personified, placed in an ordered sequence of evolution, and recited as a genealogy. The content and the sequence may vary in different island groups but, in spite of local variations, emendations, and elaborations, we see through them all the groping of the human mind to understand an ordered sequence in nature from the darkness that is dead to the light that is living. We emerge from the bondage of darkness into the light that sets us free.

Besides the antithesis between darkness and light, the concepts of plant and animal growth were dealt with in this early period by the usual techniques of personification and genealogical sequence. Plant growth is set out in some such form as follows:

> The Rootlets.
> The Tap Root.
> The Trunk.
> The Branches.
> The Twigs.
> The Leaves.

This is not only an enumeration of the parts of a tree, it also conveys the sequence in which these parts came into being.

With regard to human growth, the sequence deals with birth and adds a few personifications to indicate the development of mind wherein man differs from plants.

> Impregnation.
> Conception.
> Labor Pains.
> Bursting of [amniotic] fluid.
> Desire.
> Thought.
> Reason.

It is interesting from an evolutionary point of view that plants, fish, birds, insects, and reptiles are given as originating before man. I am not foolish enough to attempt to link this up with the Darwinian theory of evolution. It is capable of a very simple explanation. The Polynesian mythologists and storytellers used dramatic effect in their recitals, and it

was quite natural that they should enumerate plants
and animals in a sequence that led up to the climax,
man. But, in order to give man a divine origin, the
major gods had to be created before him. Hence the
periods of darkness and of light culminate in the
Sky-father and the Earth-mother, who gave birth
to the gods.

Origin of Island Groups

Before we go further, we must deal with the origin
of the island groups that were to form the habita-
tion of man. Land, as personified by the Earth-
mother, was a symbol of land in general. The island
groups that were subsequently discovered had their
own individual origin.

With the concept of an Earth-mother, it would
have been easy for the priests to have said that the
Earth-mother gave birth to children of her own kind.
But the Earth-mother had already been selected as
the mother of the gods, and evidently the mythologists at Opoa were averse to mixing the nature of
her progeny. In only one island group, Hawaii, did
the Earth-mother give birth to islands, and in this
group her motherhood of the gods has been somewhat obscured. However, it is one of three versions
concerning the origin of the islands. In the west,
Samoa and Tonga, the god Tangaroa threw down

rocks into the sea and they became islands. These concepts are sporadic and not worthy of deep-sea explorers and discoverers.

The more widely spread theories of the origin of islands are that they simply emerged from the depths of the ocean or were fished up, not by the gods but by the culture hero Maui. These theories are a metaphorical way of stressing the fact that the islands were discovered by man. In the Tahitian song concerning an ancestor named Ru, each of the islands of the leeward group of the Society Islands emerges from the sea to the drumming of the surf as Ru journeys among them. Then the drumming of the surf recedes to other neighboring groups, which emerge in the sequence given by the song. The island of Tahiti was peopled from Ra'iatea, and hence a mythical story was composed to relate that, owing to the breaking of a severe taboo in Ra'iatea, a portion of the island broke off and floated down to its present position as Tahiti. When the Polynesian navigators discovered new islands, they had to work along the surf-beaten outer reef to find some channel through which they could pass to make a landing. The song of Ru thus expresses in poetic language the discovery of islands. Similarly, the fishing up of islands is another literary expression, because the discoverer fished them up out of the unknown where

he found them. It is quite in keeping with the Polynesian trend to elaborate stories that details of bait,
hook, and line should be added to create a literary
composition. The culture hero Maui may have discovered one or more groups originally, but the story
became so popular that it was applied to islands that
Maui never saw. In the course of centuries, the metaphorical language of ancient legends has come to be
accepted literally by later generations of Polynesians.

Another myth applied to some islands is that they
were floating about and their position was afterwards
fixed by the gods, who attached them to the bottom
of the sea. This story was applied to the islands of
Aitutaki and Rarotonga in the Cook group. Tahiti
was regarded as a fish that swam to its present position from Ra'iatea; its sinews had to be cut to pre-
vent it from moving. Here again we find a literary
expression to denote the uncertain location of islands
until their locality was fixed by their human discoverers. The calling in of the gods to fix the position
was for the purpose of adding further interest by invoking the supernatural.

The Creation of Man

The religious seminary at Opoa, having constructed
a theology that accounted for the supernatural origin

of the gods, had set the stage for the creation of man. It is in keeping with Polynesian modes of thought that the material side of man, through physical birth, should come from the female and that rank and power should be inherited through the male. The gods, who had no material bodies, were faced with the problem of creating material beings to people the earth. Following the line of thought indicated above, the first created human being was a female. The gods themselves were males, and one of their number supplied the male element for the primary pair that produced the human species. This is the main scheme in the myth of human creation that was subsequently carried to the various island groups, but, in the course of time, the original story suffered local variations and contradictions.

The New Zealand version states that the major gods consulted as to how the human species should be created. The god Tane was delegated to mold some red earth at Kurawaka into the form of a woman. The figure was vitalized into the first human being. Blood flowed through her veins, she breathed, sneezed, opened her eyes, and stood erect. She was named Hine-ahu-one, the Earth-formed-maid, the human mother of mankind.

Tane took the Earth-formed-maid to wife and begat a daughter named the Dawn-maiden. The incest

that is inevitable with a primary pair took place between Tane and his daughter. Offspring were produced and the populating of the world began.

In some versions, a character named Tiki takes the
place of Tane as the male in the act of human creation with the Earth-formed-maid. Some authorities
hold that Tiki was a term used to denote the virile
power of Tane, but in other groups Tiki was regarded
as the first human male. Hence carvings in human
form are termed *tiki* in memory of the first man. In
Mangareva, where Tane is demoted to the position of
a fisherman, Tiki appears as the grandson of the god
Tangaroa, and he molds the first woman out of earth
at Ara-kovitiviti. The name given to her is Hina-one
(Earth-maid), which corresponds to the New Zealand
name. In Tahiti, a similar myth occurs with Ti'i
(Tiki) and Hina-one, but this has been overlaid by
later versions. In Hawaii, the god Kane (Tane) and
his colleagues form a man and a woman out of earth,
but the general context of the story shows that the
native historian had been influenced by the introduced
Biblical version of creation. Another Hawaiian version, however, pairs Ki'i (Tiki) with a female named
La'ila'i, as the progenitors of mankind. In the Tuamotu version, both Tiki and his wife have human ancestors. In spite of variations, the prevailing prin-
ciple is that man was born of a woman created from

earth and that the male parent was a god. Thus the New Zealanders say that the material side of man is derived from the human female ancestor, and rank, prestige, and a spark of divinity are derived from the divine male ancestor.

The myth of the Earth-formed-maid is not present in the west, in Samoa and Tonga. Here man was regarded as having developed from worms and maggots that, in turn, were developed from a rotting vine. Hence the creation of man was attributed in the west to a crude form of evolution, whereas in the rest of Polynesia it was attributed to a special creation.

War Among the Gods

A comparative study of the myths concerning the major gods reveals the fact that they were not a united family. In spite of different spheres of influence having been provided for them, they did not always live in peace and harmony with each other. The first disagreement took place before the enforced separation of the Sky-father from the Earth-mother. The separationists ranged themselves under the leadership of Tane, and the opposition, under Whiro. There was bitter opposition to Tane, which continued after the period of the separation of Rangi and Papa, but finally Whiro was defeated. In the Tahitian legends, there is a record of the struggle between Tane and the navigator Hiro. The late Queen Marau of Tahiti regarded Tane as a chief who was a contemporary of Hiro, who lived about the middle of the thirteenth century. It is thus possible that the New Zealanders have projected an historical event back into the period of the gods by confusing a human Tane with the god Tane and therefore adding his human contemporary Hiro under the dialectical form of Whiro to the godhead.

In the Tahitian traditional narratives, it is stated that the gods of Ra'iatea descended upon Tahiti and waged war against the god Tane, who was worshiped at the time in Tahiti. The principal invading god was 'Oro, the son of Ta'aroa (Tangaroa). In the end Tane was defeated. The temples of 'Oro were established in Tahiti, and 'Oro became the principal god of the Society Islands. The Cook Islands' traditions of Aitutaki, Atiu, and Mangaia state that there was an influx of people to these islands from Tahiti and that they were worshipers of the god Tane. It is thus evident that the wars between the gods were the wars between their followers and that when the worshipers of 'Oro from Ra'iatea conquered the Tahitian followers of Tane, many of the Tahitians left for the Cook Islands rather than submit to their conquerors.

From the myths and traditions of Mangaia in the Cook Islands, it would appear that the Mangaians emigrated from the neighboring island of Rarotonga. The principal god of Rarotonga was Tangaroa. The ancestors of the first settlers to Mangaia must have occupied some inferior status in Rarotonga, for they concealed their sojourn in that island and their voyage from it by saying that the island of Mangaia rose from the ocean depths with their human ancestors upon it. Not only did they shake off the temporal yoke of Rarotonga, but they emancipated themselves from the spiritual yoke of Tangaroa by substituting Rongo in his place. Thus they recast both their history and their mythology. In their mythology, they acknowledged Vatea (Atea) and Papa as the primary parents of the gods. In the family of gods, they placed Tangaroa as the first-born, with Rongo as the second, and Tane and the others following. Tangaroa was neatly disposed of by means of the custom which prevents the parents from eating with their first-born son. Vatea, in dividing his estate among his sons, proposed to give all the food to the first-born, Tangaroa. His wife, Papa, influenced by the desire to share in the food offerings, persuaded Vatea to allocate the red foods to Tangaroa and give all the other food to the second son, Rongo. Red was the color of the gods and high chieftainship, so Vatea consented. At a feast which followed, all foods with a reddish color, cooked or uncooked, were set aside in the heap for Tangaroa.

They consisted of coconuts, *taro*, fish with a reddish tinge, and crayfish and crabs that turn red on cooking. But the red foods were small in quantity, whereas the pile of other foods for Rongo was so great that some rolled off and were trodden underfoot. The symbol of chieftainship went to Tangaroa but quantity and variety went to Rongo. Tangaroa, in a huff, left and so was removed as an active member from the Mangaian pantheon. The Mangaians further concealed their mundane history by making their primary ancestors the children of the god Rongo. Hence the story of the Earth-formed-maid was omitted from Mangaian mythology. It is interesting to note that the Mangaians added the Rarotongan ancestor Tangiia to their gods but projected him back in time by making him a brother of Tangaroa and Rongo.

In Mangareva, the principal god was Tu, but he was made the eldest son of Tangaroa instead of his brother. Atea was present as one of the earliest gods but he appeared as an individual and not the father of the gods.

It is evident from the mythology of different island groups that a pattern of theology was carried out from the center to the marginal islands along the various radials. The main feature consisted of a number of deified ancestors having been grouped together into one family by making them the children of personifications of Space and Earth. The gods were given separate departments to rule over, but, though they were theoretically equal, different island groups have had the tendency to exalt one member of the family over the others. Thus Tangaroa was exalted in the Society and Cook Islands, Tane in New Zealand and Hawaii, Rongo in Mangaia, and Tu in Mangareva. In the process of exalting a particular god above his fellows, the older pattern of mythology was sometimes altered to fit the circumstances, as in the supplanting of the elder brother Tangaroa by Rongo in Mangaia. The struggle among the gods for greater prestige was merely a reflection of what took place among their human followers.

Later Elaboration in Ra'iatea

A study in Tahitian theology reveals the fact that, after the family of gods had radiated from Taputapu-atea with the colonizing ships, further elaboration took place at that center of religious teaching. The priests who supported Ta'aroa (Tangaroa) seemed to have gained the ascendancy, for the cult of Ta'aroa was spread from Ra'iatea to Tahiti and forced upon the followers of Tane in that island. An early stage of this cult spread as far as Rarotonga in the Cook Islands, for Tangaroa there was merely the principal god and not a creator. At Taputapu-atea, however,

Ta'aroa was elevated to the position of Creator, and the old pattern of mythology was changed accordingly. This is the new tale that the priestly scholars elaborated:

"Ta'aroa, the Creator, was self-begotten, for he had no father and no mother. He sat in a shell named Rumia, shaped like an egg, for countless ages in endless space in which there was no sky, land, sea, moon, nor stars. This was the period of continuous, countless darkness and thick impenetrable darkness. At long last Ta'aroa cracked the shell to hatch himself. He stood on the shell and called in various directions, but no sound answered from the void. He retired within Rumia into an inner shell termed Lesser-foundation, where he lay torpid for a further untold period. At last he determined to act. He emerged and made the inner shell of Rumia into a foundation for the rock and soil of the world, and the outer shell he made into the dome of the sky which was low and confined. He breathed into the rock foundation the essence of himself and personified it as Tumu-nui to be the husband; likewise he personified the rock stratum as Papa-raharaha to be the wife. . . . Then Ta'aroa created rock, sand, and Earth. He conjured up Tu, the great craftsman, to help him in the task of creation, and together they formed the myriad roots. The dome of Rumia was raised on pillars, and thus space beneath was extended. The space was termed *atea* and pervaded with a spirit personified as Atea. Land and space were increased, and the under-world was set apart. Forest trees and food plants grew, and living things appeared on the land and in the sea. At the back were the mountains personified as Tu-mou'a, with land, springs, and rivers. In front was the ocean and its rocks ruled by the ocean lord Tino-rua. Above was Atea (Space) and below was Rua (Abyss). The land was Havai'i, the birthplace of other lands, gods, kings, and man.

"Darkness brooded under the confined dome of Rumia. The gods Tu, Atea, Uru, and others were created or conjured forth by Ta'aroa in darkness. From Ta'aroa and Atea (here a female) the god Tane was born. Rongo was born from a cloud and then Atea changed sex to become a male." *

This version of Ta'aroa's existing in a shell shaped like an egg and then emerging as a creator exists only in the Society Islands and was evidently composed at Taputapu-atea after the colonists had left for other islands. It places Ta'aroa at the beginning of the evolutionary period of natural phenomena to predate the Sky-father Atea. Atea is further demoted by changing his sex to female and making him the mother of Tane. The older myth is then reverted to by re-

* P. H. Buck (Te Rangi Hiroa), *Vikings of the Sunrise,* p. 69.

storing his original sex. Competition from the powerful Tane is further disposed of by making him the
son of Ta'aroa and Atea, while the other major gods,
Tu and Rongo, are simply conjured forth by Ta'aroa.
Thus did the priests of Opoa consolidate in heaven
the victory they had won on earth.

A later elaboration was the creation of 'Oro as the
son of Ta'aroa. Ta'aroa was retired as an emeritus,
and his son 'Oro became the active functioning god at
the temple of Taputapu-atea. Again the Ra'iatean
fleets sailed to Tahiti to proselytize the people. After
severe fighting, 'Oro was imposed on the Tahitians,
and a new temple named Taputapu-atea was erected
for his worship in the district of Tautira. In time, 'Oro
became the principal god of the Society Islands but
his worship spread no farther. The name of 'Oro as a
son of Ta'aroa does not occur in the myths and genealogies of any island group but the Society Islands.
This limited distribution supports my contention that
'Oro was a late addition to the Society Islands' pantheon.

The promotion of Ta'aroa as a creator did not do
away with the worship of other gods. He was merely
supreme among many, and the remade theology remained polytheistic.

We have seen that the early polytheistic pattern
evolved at Ra'iatea was carried in its original sim-

plicity to New Zealand, but local additions were made to the family of the Sky-father and the Earth-mother. A notable addition was that of Haumea as the god of uncultivated food. The name of Haumea is present in other island myths but appears usually as a female who has no connection with uncultivated food. The new function of Haumea in New Zealand was due to certain local conditions that did not occur on the volcanic islands of the tropics. The New Zealand climate was so much colder than that of Polynesia that the coconut, breadfruit, plantain, and banana would not grow, and even the introduced sweet potato, *taro*, and yam were restricted to the warmer parts of the islands. This curtailment in cultivated food supplies rendered the endemic bracken fern (*Pteris aquilina* var. *esculenta*) very important. The underground rhizome of this plant was rich in carbohydrates, and, being widely spread, it became a more constant and a surer source of carbohydrate food than the introduced plants. The god of the introduced food plants was Rongo, but, as the bracken fern was recognized as growing wild in the new country, the care of this uncultivated food was given to Haumea. As Haumea was added to a male pantheon, the sex was apparently accepted as being male. Hence local conditions have had an influence on the personnel of the family of the gods.

Monotheism

In addition, however, to changes in and additions to the old pattern, there is evidence that an esoteric school arose in some part of New Zealand, probably in the Wairarapa district of the North Island. Like the religious seminary at Taputapu-atea, the New Zealand school created a creator but gave him the name of Io. Like Ta'aroa, Io had no parents but simply came into being. He was then made responsible for the creation of the already existing pattern of religion, but certain additions were made. Two more skies were added to the older count of ten, and Io went into residence in the twelfth, or topmost, sky. A house was provided for him, named Rangiatea, and the assembly place before it was named Te Rauroha. A staff of Celestial Maids (Mareikura) was provided, and Guardians (Poutiriao) were appointed to the series of sky levels which were given individual names. Messengers were engaged to carry on communication between Io and the major gods who were not interfered with in the new reorganization. As Io was regarded as the source of all knowledge, a new incident was added in Tane's ascending to the topmost heaven to obtain the three baskets of knowledge from Io. An old incident was introduced when Whiro tried to oppose Tane's mis-

sion but Tane was eventually victorious. It will be
seen that the New Zealand revision was much more
smoothly accomplished than that at Taputapu-atea.
Furthermore, there is no evidence that the Maori
school attempted to proselytize other tribes. The cult
of Io seems to have been an intellectual effort confined to the higher priesthood and to have a limited
distribution. Except for the element of predating a
creator, there is no similarity in the details of the cults
of Io and Ta'aroa. Io steps into the picture as a new
individual with a higher prestige than the major gods,
but the religion of the people remained polytheistic.

A third center of religious activity resulting in
drastic changes appears in the Tuamotu atolls. From
native informants and from his translations of various chants, J. F. Stimson has come to the belief that
the Tuamotuans also had a creator named Kiho or
Kio. Kio fights with Atea and others for supremacy
and conquers them. It is tempting to see a similarity
between Kio and Io, but, as the Maoris do not drop
the consonant k, they seem to be distinct words. Furthermore, an analysis of the details of the Tuamotuan
and New Zealand myths show nothing in common beyond the promotion of an individual above his fellows.
Here again the religion remained polytheistic.

There has been a tendency to regard these sporadic
occurrences of a creator as evidence that the Poly-

nesians originally had a monotheistic religion which was later changed to polytheism. From the pattern of Polynesian society, which in turn influenced the religious pattern, we see that the dominant features are the distribution and sharing of food and material goods and the budding off into family groups ruled by their own chiefs. The offerings of food and the division of power among a number of gods follow the human pattern. At the same time, there was a constant struggle for supreme power among the chiefs, and this struggle was reflected in the various island groups in the wars of the gods for supremacy. I believe that Polynesian religion has always been polytheistic but that intellectuals among the priesthood have in some localities elevated a particular god to supremacy among his fellows by making him a creator. I regard these versions of a creator as late sporadic efforts that took place after the general dispersal and not as the remnants of an ancient general monotheism.

Summary

We have seen that in a simple stage of social development man created his gods. The parents of the gods were human beings who had their place in the family genealogy. The technique of deification was continued by family groups until the advent of Christianity.

There is a certain affinity between gods and eponymous ancestors whose names were used to denote tribes and subtribes. The major gods and tribal ancestors were earlier in time and were shared by many, whereas the minor gods and subtribal ancestors were later in time and were shared by a lesser number of people.

With the passing of years and the growth of an intellectual and imaginative priesthood, some of the deified ancestors who had led the great voyages into central Polynesia were given a greater prestige by changing a human parentage into a supernatural origin to fit in with a reconstructed theology. The abandoned and forgotten human parents were replaced by the personifications of the Sky-father and the Earth-mother. Additional prestige was given to these major gods by reversing the earlier technique and making them the creators of man. Thus man-created gods in their turn created man.

III

THE DEATH OF THE GODS

Introduction

THE Polynesian families created their household
gods and then, under the guidance of the priesthood, the gods created the Polynesians. The loves,
wars, and adventures of the gods would fill as many
volumes as the similar activities of the gods of Greece,
Rome, or Scandinavia. The priests composed a theology, but the textile was so interwoven with the
threads of society that it was doomed to decay on con-
tact with Western civilization.

The first foreigners to initiate outside change were
the early voyagers and traders. They brought metal
tools and loom-woven cloth to a stone-age people. The
superiority of metals over stone was so obvious that
the Polynesians were seized with the frantic desire to
obtain the new trade goods at any cost. They stole and
they bartered their own material goods, food, and
even their women to satisfy the new needs that had
been created. On the trail of the voyagers and traders
came the missionaries of a new religion. They were
more or less permanent settlers. Though they came
primarily to convert the heathen, they brought West-

ern goods not only for their own use but to barter with the natives. It was the material goods of this world that appealed primarily to the natives and not the hope of reward after death. Material benefit was associated with the new religion and, if such benefits could be obtained more readily by adopting that religion, why not adopt it? The Polynesians deserted their gods and sold them for a mess of pottage.

The desertion of the Polynesian gods was not so difficult as it may seem. The people had created new family gods all down the ages and, as a consequence, had deserted and forgotten older creations. When sickness afflicted the worshipers of the god Tane in Tahiti, they blamed their god and upbraided him as the god with yellow fangs who was eating his followers. A priest of Tane placed the sennit symbol of the god in a coconut shell, plugged the opening, and set it afloat in the sea to seek a new home in a distant land. Later the priest set sail to seek his god. After visiting various islands unsuccessfully, he came to the island of Mangaia in the Cook group. Here he built a temple, and with a scoop net he sought a fish as an offering on the new temple. In addition to a small fish, he caught up the coconut shell that he had set adrift in Tahiti. He removed the plug, and the sennit symbol within announced its presence with a chirp—*kio*. The evicted

god was reëstablished on the new temple as Tane-kio,
Tane-the-chirper.

Defeat in war was often attributed to lack of power
of the war god, and sometimes the inadequate god was
deposed and another set up in his place. The god of
the victors was often imposed upon the conquered,
as when the god 'Oro from the island of Ra'iatea was
imposed upon the followers of Tane in Tahiti. The
acceptance of a more powerful god as a means of ob-
taining temporal power was a common Polynesian
characteristic.

In the proselytizing of Polynesia by the London
Missionary Society, instances occur in which the desertion of the Polynesian gods was aided by events
that occurred within the native culture itself. When
the first representatives of the Society went to Tahiti
in 1798, they stayed in the district ruled over by the
chief Pomare. The selection of the district was influenced by the fact that the navigators Wallis and Cook
had landed there and regarded Pomare as the king of
Tahiti. In reality, Pomare was but chief of the district
and there were more powerful chiefs in other districts.
As first the missionaries had very little success in the
conversion of the people, though the material goods
they brought were much appreciated. The missionaries
were opposed, and many of them left the island in

despair. When a fresh set of missionaries arrived some years later, Pomare was in a more chastened frame of mind. He had been defeated in battle and had taken refuge on the neighboring island of Mo'orea. The missionaries accompanied him there and began to make headway with him. Pomare had begun to distrust his gods because of his lack of success against his enemies. He began to flirt with the missionaries in the hope that their god was more powerful than his own and would bring him the military success he wanted. At the same time, he was chary of abandoning his own gods entirely. Thus, though the missionaries had hopes of converting Pomare, they could not get him to abandon his gods publicly. In view of the prospects, however, the missionaries ranged themselves on the side of Pomare and regarded his enemies as "heathen." In 1815, Pomare's enemies on the island of Tahiti invited him to attend a conference with them. Pomare, accompanied by his supporters and some of the missionaries, sailed over to Tahiti and, on a Sunday morning, he and his people attended a service conducted by the missionaries. During the service, the enemy was observed advancing with a large armed force, evidently to attack. The congregation became alarmed and the missionaries were prepared to break off the service. Pomare, however, ordered the service to be continued to its proper ending and stated that the enemy could be attended to afterwards. The missionary writer, Reverend W. Ellis,* had praised Pomare's piety and faith in continuing the service in the face of the enemy. The truth is that any religious ritual that was broken off was regarded by the Polynesians as an ill omen for future success. The gods being invoked for assistance turned against their worshipers if the ritual was not properly completed. It was not Christian piety that induced Pomare to go on with the service but the Polynesian fear of a broken ritual. At the end of the service both Pomare and his followers had plucked up courage in the hope that the Christian god would assist them in gaining the victory.

From the outset of the battle which ensued, fortune smiled on Pomare. The opposing leader, whose rank was immeasurably superior to that of Pomare, was killed with a musket ball. On the death of their leader, the enemy retired and victory lay with Pomare and with the Christian god who had supported him. The power of Jehovah having been demonstrated, Christianity was accepted by the whole island of Tahiti, and Pomare became king of the group. Pomare handed over the material symbols of his native gods to the missionaries to be sent to England to show the people of that country what fools the Tahitians had been. A

* Reverend W. Ellis, *Polynesian Researches* (London, 1829).

lucky shot had done more than seventeen years of preaching had been able to accomplish.

The gospel was carried to the island of Aitutaki in 1823, and for two years the native missionaries from Tahiti made no headway. Then the favorite granddaughter of a high chief took seriously ill. The high chief made offerings on his temple to his gods, and the priests performed all the native ritual in invoking the gods to restore the child to health. All was to no avail, and the child died. The high chief was so enraged that he sent his son with a lighted torch to set fire to the gods and the sacred buildings on the temple. The high chief felt that his gods had deserted him in his hour of need, so he abandoned them with a drastic demonstration. He then turned to the gods of the missionaries. The native missionary was quick to take advantage of the incident, and he preached a powerful sermon showing the futility of the native gods. The native population was caught up in a wave of emotional reaction, and throughout the island the gods were destroyed and the temples defaced and desecrated. A few images and sacred objects, shorn of their divinity, were sent to London to demonstrate the success that was attending the missionary efforts.

To illustrate in more detail what happened to the native mores and culture after the Polynesian gods were deserted, I am going to take the island of Mangaia in the Cook group as a concrete example of the collapse that occurred.

Mangaian Gods

The national god of Mangaia, worshiped by all the tribes, was Rongo, a son of the Sky-father and the Earth-mother. The ritual to Rongo was conducted on two temples, one inland of the great upraised coral reef that surrounded the island and the other on the shore side of the upraised reef. The shore temple, named Orongo, contained a large stone image of Rongo and a smaller stone image standing behind it. Human sacrifices were offered to Rongo at the ceremony of installing the commander of a victorious tribe as Military Dictator of the island. After the ceremony, peace was declared over the land by sounding drums on the temple.

Each tribe had its own tribal god with a temple in its tribal district. One of these gods was Tane, a brother of Rongo. A symbol carved in wood represented each god, and these, to the number of thirteen, were kept in a special god house that stood between two important inland temples. They were tended by a hereditary keeper who kept them wrapped in special coverings of thick white bark cloth and fed them with offerings of *taro* every evening.

In addition to the important temples, there were shrines on the coast consisting of stones erected to the two gods of fishermen. One, near the shore residence of the Shore-high-priest, was to Rua-tama'ine. Attached to a stake beside it was an open basket in which the fortunate fisherman deposited a portion of his catch as a present to the Shore-high-priest and as an offering to Rua-tama'ine. The stone representing the other god, Rua'atu, received an offering of a small fish from the successful fisherman and a coral pebble from the unsuccessful.

Priests

Of the priesthood, the most important were the two high priests of Rongo. One, termed the Inland-high-priest (Ariki-pa-uta), conducted the ritual at the inland temple of Rongo; the other, termed the Shore-high-priest (Ariki-pa-tai), conducted the ceremonies at the shore temple of Orongo. Both these priests were of the highest rank and their offices were hereditary. They were descended from Rangi and 'Akatauira, two of the three original settlers of Mangaia.

A third high priest was responsible for the distribution of food on public occasions. He rejoiced in the title of the Ariki-i-te-ua-i-te-tapora-kai, the High-chief-who-stood-at-the-head-of-the-food-platter. He also conducted the correct ritual at the shore before the fleet set out for the fishing grounds. It was his office to give each canoe a plaited symbol of coconut leaflets representing Mokoiro, a deified patron of fishermen. The symbol was placed in the bow of the canoe and brought success. The office was hereditary and its holders claimed direct descent from Mokoiro, the third of the original settlers of Mangaia.

In addition to these three national priests, each of the thirteen tribes had its own tribal priest who served as the medium between the tribal group and their god. He conducted services on the local temple in the tribal district, and offerings of food were made to insure success on tribal ventures. Each priest also had a part of his dwelling house curtained off with a large sheet of bark cloth. Within this sacred chamber, a material form of the god was kept. The priest could consult his god privately within the curtained recess, but public services had to be conducted on the open temple. On the temple courtyard, small houses were erected to serve as temporary residences for the gods during certain rituals. The office of tribal priest was hereditary and he exercised great power.

A custom with religious significance was that of cutting the navel cord of a newly born child. The navel cord was not cut until the afterbirth had come away. The person who cut the cord cleared away the coagulated blood in the part severed. Before cutting, he asked the parents the name of the god to whom the child should be dedicated. Marriage usually took place between people of different tribes. Hence the father and mother of a child worshiped different tribal gods. It was usual for the father to give the name of his tribal god, but sometimes, when the mother's tribe was in the ascendancy, the name of her god was given. The operator then announced, "I hereby cleanse the cord of this child to —," giving the name of the god.

This religious presentation led to the establishment of the office of an official cutter of navel cords, who was termed a *vaekai*. The *vaekai* received presents of food and goods for his services, and the cutting of the cord by a *vaekai* conferred social distinction on the person so treated. The commoners, who were not in the position to employ a *vaekai*, had their cords cut by ordinary individuals, and social distinction was denied them.

Social Customs

Certain matters concerned with social organization must be mentioned to complete the picture. The Mangaians differ somewhat from their neighbors in the other Cook Islands in the emphasis they gave to success in war. In the numerous wars that took place, the leader of the victorious tribe was publicly installed as the Military Dictator of the island. He was regarded as having secured the *Mangaia*, which is not only the name of the island but refers also to absolute temporal power. His installation was marked by the offering of a human sacrifice to the god Rongo on the inland temple where the Inland-high-priest officiated. After this first ceremony, the human sacrifice was carried to the shore temple of Orongo, where the Shore-high-priest formally installed the victor in his office of Dictator. The Dictator then named his supporting chiefs as chiefs over districts and subdistricts in the conquered area and also in his own territory. They were installed with public announcement by the Shore-high-priest, who gave each a portion of flesh from the human offering. These were then taken back to the districts and offered on the local temples to insure a successful rule and the fertility of the land. Drums were beaten on the temple of Orongo by a hereditary drum beater and his family. There was a procession around the island, during which the drums were beaten on each district temple in turn. The drums announced the cessation of war, and the survivors of the defeated tribe emerged from their hiding places in safety. The hereditary drum beater received a grant of land from the new administration.

The Constitution

In the history of Mangaia, the fortunes of war wavered among the tribes of the different districts. The vanquished of yesterday were the victors of to-

day, and the victors of today were the vanquished of
tomorrow. The successful tribe enjoyed the rich food
lands, and the conquered eked out a bare existence in
the narrow upland valleys and the recesses of the
raised coral reef known as the *makatea*. A change of
government could be brought about only by success in
battle. The conquered, under this system, cherished
the hope of building up their forces by tribal increase
or by making an alliance with other tribes to regain
power by the arbitrament of war.

Let us now consider how this complex culture, which
was the result of a gradual adjustment and evolution
extending over a number of centuries, was rudely shat-
tered when the Mangaians deserted their own gods.
Just as a hereditary chief was dependent upon his
tribesmen for maintaining power and authority, so
the gods were dependent upon the continued support
of their worshipers. When the Mangaians deserted
their gods in favor of Christianity, they destroyed
them as surely as if they had been mortal beings.

Advent of Missionaries

In 1823, three native missionaries from Tahiti with
the wives of two of them were landed at Mangaia from
a London Missionary Society's schooner. They received such rough treatment at the hands of the Mangaians that they all swam back to the ship's boat

which had waited outside the reef to see the reception. An epidemic of dysentery broke out on the island soon after the visit, and the natives attributed it to the anger of the visitors' god. Two other missionaries, Davida and Tiare, were landed at the island in the following year. The Mangaians, afraid of incurring another epidemic of dysentery, afforded them protection, built them a house, and allowed them to expound their faith to those who would listen to them.

It had so happened that in the last war the combined tribes of Ngati-tane and Ngati-manahune had defeated the existing government of Ngati-vara. The Shore-high-priest, whose sympathies were with the defeated Ngati-vara, entered politics and refused to assist in the installation of the victorious leader, Pangemiro. Pangemiro promptly deposed the Shore-high-priest from office and combined the position with that of the Inland-high-priest, held by one Numangatini. The ritual of installation could not be carried out properly, but Pangemiro functioned as Dictator. Pangemiro died three years later and, as there had been no war, the office of Dictator fell into temporary abeyance. The highest ranking chief was Numangatini, holding the offices of both Inland-high-priest and Shore-high-priest.

It was at this peculiar stage that the two Tahitian missionaries landed on Mangaia and came under the protection of the dominant Ngati-tane tribe. In the course of time they made converts among the Ngati-tane, and finally the chiefs of the Ngati-tane and the Ngati-manahune accepted the new religion. The converted males marked their conversion by cutting off their long hair, and the taboos that prevented the sexes eating together and parents eating with their first-born sons were abolished. The national god house was burned to the ground, and the gods that had reposed in it were thrown in a heap before the missionaries. The coverings of bark cloth were removed and cast into the sea. By exposing the gods to the vulgar gaze, they were dishonored. The temples were desecrated by the burning of the god houses on them. Led by the native missionaries, the work of destruction went on, and even the groves of noble trees that gave shelter to the temples were felled to the ground.

The Ngati-vara, who remained in opposition, were horrified and went into mourning. Dressed in evil-smelling bark cloth that had been soaked in the mud of *taro* swamps, and with faces and bodies blackened with charcoal, they formed a sad procession around the island as a protest against the desertion of the gods of Mangaia.

The new religion preached brotherly love and the cessation of war. The cessation of war was agreeable to the tribes in power at the time, for its acceptance meant that they would enjoy power forever, but to the defeated tribes it meant that they must give up all chance of ever regaining the government and recovering the fertile food lands they had lost. Hence the victorious Ngati-tane and Ngati-manahune readily became Christians, but the defeated Ngati-vara, by refusing to depart from the original constitution, remained "heathen." The missionaries, perhaps without fully realizing it, were political propagandists.

Matters reached a head when the Ngati-vara assembled their forces and offered battle to regain government over the island. European missionary writers have described the event as a struggle between the Christians and the "heathens," but to the anthropologist the struggle was not religious but political. The Ngati-vara were using the only cultural means available to them to change the government. Had they accepted Christianity, they would have given up the only means of effecting change. The Ngati-tane, on the other hand, had followed the course adopted by Pomare in Tahiti in hoping that the missionaries' god would be powerful enough to keep them in power. During the battle, the Tahitian missionary, Davida, remained on his knees, supplicating Jehovah to grant victory to the Ngati-tane; in a thatched hut perched on a high rock, Tereavai, priest of the Ngati-vara, invoked his tribal god Te A'ia to give success to their arms. The spiritual power of Te A'ia, however, had departed with that of the other Polynesian gods, and the heathen were defeated. The Ngati-vara were offered food lands if they would accept the new religion and live in Christian villages. The terms were accepted, though for some time a large number refused to conform to the outward visible signs of an inward spiritual grace. These Christians also signalized their conversion by cutting off their long hair, and the women wore garments of white bark cloth instead of the brown color previously in fashion.

Cultural Revolution

Though the Polynesians in the past had abandoned some gods in favor of others, the substitutions and incidental changes were made in the same basic culture. The process of change proceeded along lines of natural growth and evolution. In the substitution of Jehovah for Rongo and the tribal gods, the Christian complex of a foreign culture displaced elements in the native culture that were associated not only with religion but with the organization of society and the arts and crafts. The results of the clash that occurred between two different cultures were revolutionary.

Religious Changes

When the Christian iconoclasts gained their victory over their opponents, the native ceremonial following a victory could not be observed. Through the acceptance of the Christian tenets, a human sacrifice could not be offered to Rongo. Without a human sacrifice, the correct ceremonies for installing a new government could not be conducted on the inland and shore temples of Rongo. Numangatini, by transferring his allegiance to Jehovah, could not carry out his duties to Rongo, for which duties the two offices he held had been created. The peace drums could not be sounded. Hence the high priestly offices of the Inland-high-priest and the Shore-high-priest ceased to function. Though Numangatini bore the double title, the function of publicly interceding with the gods for the welfare of the people and the fertility of food supplies had been automatically transferred to the Tahitian missionary, the foreign priest of Jehovah.

The high office of the Distributor of Food also was shorn of its religious significance. The charms that gave success to the fishing fleets were no longer made, for the patron deity, Mokoiro, was deserted as was Rongo; his priest was displaced by the native missionary from a distant island. Now before the fishing fleet

set out, the fishermen bent their knees on the seashore
while the missionary, Davida, offered up a Christian
prayer for success.

The hereditary priests of the tribal gods also joined
the ranks of the unemployed. The expert craftsmen,
who carved the gods out of wood and made the special
thick bark cloth to clothe them, lost their employment
and their status in society. The keeper of the national
god house lost his position, for the house was burned
to the ground and the gods defiled. The beater of the
drum and his family were deprived of their office of
making drums and sounding them to usher in peace,
for the ritual was abandoned and with it went the
gifts of land that pertained to their office. Gods, temples, and ritual were swept away in one fell swoop, and
the hereditary offices of three high priests, thirteen
tribal priests, and two subsidiary offices disappeared
with them.

The food basket of the fish deity, Rua-tama'ine,
was no longer hung up near the now-deserted house
of the deposed Shore-high-priest. The fishing festivals
in honor of first-born sons and first-born daughters
could no longer be observed, for they had been accompanied by offerings of fish to the tribal gods. The individual fisherman dropped not a pebble and spoke
not a word as he passed the stone shrine of Rua'atu.
The avalanche that had swept away his major deities

swept away the minor deities as well. He had been taught by the new priest that Jehovah was a jealous god and "Thou shalt serve no other gods but me."

The change from a polytheistic to a monotheistic system made the gods of the father and mother identical. The child's navel cord had to be cut as a physical necessity, but the process was divested of its religious significance. The cord was no longer cut to the tribal god of the father, and the child could no longer boast of the social distinction given by having his cord treated by a *vaekai* expert. The official cutter of cords joined the ranks of the unemployed. The missionary priest of the one god had supplanted him, and the ritual of admission was changed to the making of the sign of the cross on the infant's forehead with a finger dipped in water.

The new religion required assembly places for its converts, and the large houses of worship of another culture took the place of the stone inclosures that had been defaced and desecrated. The roofed church displaced the open temple, and within its entrance stood the font indicating that admission to the service of the new god was by baptism with water and not by the cutting of the navel cord. The ritual within the new building was conducted by the missionary Davida and his successors. The multiple duties that had been carried out on various temples by a number of priests of rank and power were dispensed with, and the new forms were the monopoly of a single missionary. Ancient offices that had been inherited from illustrious ancestors were swept away, and a visiting missionary, appointed by the white representatives of the London Missionary Society, took their place. *Sic transit gloria Mangaiae.*

A few more changes took place as a direct result of the new religion. Prayers and hymns supplanted the chants and incantations of the old religion. The ancient ritual had formed what may be termed the immaterial property of the priestly families. It had been of immense value to them but, as its value disappeared, the ancient chants were no longer taught and were soon forgotten.

The Bible was translated into the Rarotongan dialect, and one of the white missionaries stated with pride, "The Bible is read, studied, and quoted by the Polynesians of today *in place of* the heathen songs and myths of bygone ages." * The learned natives, termed *'are korero,* ceased to transmit orally the Mangaian myths, legends, and traditions, for they had ceased to be of academic value. What has filtered through are woefully attenuated versions often distorted to conform more closely to the Biblical stories

* W. W. Gill, *From Darkness to Light in Polynesia* (London, 1894), p. 253.

with which the minds of native informants had become saturated.

The Mangaian version of the future state consisted of an underworld for the souls of those who died an ordinary death and a special region in the heavens, termed Tai'iria, for those who died in battle. In the underworld, an ogress named Miru received captured souls and cooked them in an oven, not as punishment for evil in this world but simply because she was a female cannibal. It was easy for the Mangaians to accept the new theory of a hell in the underworld with an everlasting fire to punish the nonconverted. A heaven in the upper spaces as a reward for the Christians supplanted the Tai'iria of the favored warriors.

The frequent human sacrifices were replaced by the one supreme sacrifice of Jesus Christ, and the symbolism of the holy sacrament struck a reminiscent chord.

The teaching that Jehovah created the world in six days and the subsequent taboo of every seventh day as a day of rest were accepted literally by the Mangaians. The institution of the Sabbath led to the abandonment of the annual lunar cycle with months determined by the rising of the new moon with each night named after the phases of the moon. Its place was taken by the Christian solar year divided into twelve calendar months with their subdivision into weeks, each culminating in a sacred Sabbath. The taboo of the Sabbath was such that all the food for the Sabbath was cooked on the preceding Saturday. All work on the Sabbath was tabooed, and even walking to other villages on Sunday was punished by a fine of five dollars.

Social Changes

In addition to religious changes, the new religion effected drastic changes in social matters. At the last battle between the converted and the unconverted, Numangatini with the combined offices of two high priests was the highest ranking chief on the Christian side. He was regarded as having acquired the position of Dictator, but he could not be installed with the ancient rites that had been abandoned on the acceptance of Christianity. However, he was regarded by the converted Christians and the missionaries as the king of Mangaia. Hence a new title was created and, war having been ended by the last battle, the office became hereditary instead of depending on the varying fortunes of battle. Similarly, the offices of district and subdistrict chiefs also became hereditary instead of being redistributed after each conquest.

After the way had been paved by the native Tahitian missionary, a white missionary took up his residence in Mangaia, and three native pastors were appointed to minister to the increasing number of converts. The manner in which the missionaries had taken precedence in social matters is shown by the order of precedence in calling the distribution of food at the public feasts. In the original culture, the order was: (1) tribal priests, (2) high priests, (3) military dictator, (4) district and subdistrict chiefs. In the new society, the order was (1) white missionary, (2) three native pastors, (3) king, and (4) district and subdistrict chiefs.

A drastic change was also introduced in the native marriage customs. In the native culture, the chiefs could have more than one wife, and they could add a wife's sister to the ménage. It was also considered the correct thing for a man to marry his brother's widow and so keep her children in the deceased's family. In the old order, the marriage was made by the mutual consent of the two families concerned and there was no religious ceremony. The new order demanded that all marriages should be conducted with a religious ceremony by the church and, furthermore, that only one wife be allowed. Men with plural wives were ordered to select one and abandon the others, even though they had had children by them. Some heart-rending separations took place for, if the husband did not make his choice, he was refused admission to the church by adult baptism. The one marriage was legalized by a church service. If a church member took back another wife, he was excommunicated by the church and ostracized by the church members. As a result of monogamy, the sororate custom disappeared, for a man could not take his wife's sister while his wife was alive. The levirate custom also was abandoned because, even for the sake of fatherless orphans, a man could not take his brother's widow into his household if he already had a wife. The restriction to one god was accompanied by a restriction to one wife. In the native culture, there was no connection between gods and wives.

Furthermore, the native marriages were arranged by parents on either side, with due regard to family alliances and to keeping the chiefly stock pure. The church, however, stepped in and refused to marry any couple until they had discovered the real wishes of the pair to be married. If a young couple disagreed with their parents, the church opposed the wishes of the parents and thus helped to break down parental and family control.

The church, as guided by the white missionaries, appears to have regarded most of the ancient customs as relics of heathenism and therefore to be abolished. One of the white missionaries, on going to the church to marry a couple, found the bridegroom's tribe lying stretched across the road for a distance of a hundred yards, while the intended bride tripped merrily over their bodies on the way to the church. She was being honored by her prospective husband's tribe with the ancient custom termed *maninitori*. However, the missionary could see nothing in it but the revival of a heathen custom and, as punishment, he postponed the marriage until the following day.

Code of Laws

The taboos that belonged to the native culture were abolished, and a new set of taboos was imposed in a code of laws which, among other things, was aimed at regulating relations between the sexes. The whole nature of the Mangaians was to be changed by a system of punishments that would suppress their natural desires. The punishments consisted of fines, of which part was paid in cash and part in trade goods. To curtail the opportunities for clandestine meetings, the curfew bell was introduced, and any persons found outside their houses after 8.00 P.M. were fined.

Some of the laws dealing with sex matters, as translated from the missionary laws of Mangaia, were as follows:

Fornication. Fine: One dollar cash and fourteen dollars trade.

Village conduct. If a man puts his arm around a woman in the road at night, and he has a torch in his hand, he shall go free. If no torch, to be fined one dollar cash and nine dollars trade.

Tattooing love marks. The man who does this on a woman or the woman who does this on a man shall be fined two dollars cash and thirteen dollars trade.

Taking woman inland. If a man takes a woman to the mountains for bad purposes, he is to be fined fifteen dollars—one in cash and fourteen in trade.

Crying after a dead woman. If a man do this, and he and the woman were not relatives, or if he wear mourning for her, he is to be fined fifteen dollars—one in cash and fourteen in trade.

These fines may not seem very high in these days, but they meant a great deal at the period when they were in force.

With the introduction of a system foreign to native culture came also the foreign technique for enforcing the laws. Police were appointed to detect lawbreakers, and judges were appointed to inflict fines. These officials were selected from the deacons and members of the church. The fines, like ancient Gaul, were divided into three parts: one went to the king, one to the judge, and one to the police. The fines constituted the whole salary of the officials, and it is but natural that the police should have hailed as many people as possible before the judge. The police force increased in an extraordinary manner. In 1891, for a population of 1,860 there were 155 police, or one policeman to every 12 inhabitants. The enforcement of the moral laws led to a regular system of espionage on the private life of the people. The police visited the various houses after the curfew sounded and at irregular intervals during the night. The absence of residents, particularly young people, was held as positive proof of clandestine love affairs, and the absentees were promptly fined the next day. The deacons and elders who did not happen to be in the police force felt it their duty to report cases of suspicious conduct.

Though the Mangaians had adopted a code of laws, they had not been instructed in the fundamentals of British justice. They did not understand that an accused person is not guilty until full evidence on both sides has been submitted to the judge and a conviction made on that evidence. In the imperfectly understood system that was adopted, the accused was convicted by the police, and the judge held office not to weigh the evidence impartially but to inflict the fine automatically. Both police and judge desired as many convictions as possible in order to share the greater spoil. In other words, the system degenerated into a racket, which was made possible by the introduction of something totally foreign to native culture—money.

Adolescents and young unmarried people could not wholly grasp the moral sin in obeying the physiological urge of nature, whereas the elders of the church, whose sex life was practically over, were ready to punish those who took advantage of opportunities of which they could no longer avail themselves. To the younger people the sin was the sin of being found out, and so they bent their faculties to the sport of evading the police. When caught, they paid their fines without any feeling of moral delinquency.

Both native pastors and white missionaries experienced additional difficulties that did not emanate from the native people whom they had persuaded to desert their own gods. The natives naturally inferred that the Christian religion was the religion of the white man. But, though they themselves were subjected to a severe code of theocratic laws, the white sailors and traders who followed on the heels of the missionaries were by no means willing to conform to it. They broke the moral law by living with native women without going through the initial stage of marriage by the church. They introduced alcohol and gambling with cards, things hitherto unknown in the island. The code of laws was therefore amended to include fines against drunkenness and gambling. In addition to their own failings, the natives were burdened with the failings of civilization.

Though other laws were framed for a good purpose, I have stressed that aspect of the code that interfered with the private life of the people in a somewhat unwarrantable manner. With the establishment of government control from New Zealand as late as 1900 A.D., the theocratic code of laws was amended, and the people have had time to adjust themselves to a more reasonable rule.

Songs, Dances

The new religion established further laws or taboos against the recreations of the people. The missionary Gill, in discussing the dances that accompanied the old-time dramatic performances, stated: *

"But the dance itself was invariably connected with very serious evils; so that on the establishment of Christianity, it was abolished."

Gill further explains the evils: †

"The chiefs, whether married or not, often wore phallic ear ornaments." Thus, to abolish the ornaments, the missionaries abolished the dance.

The dramatic songs that accompanied the dances were also forbidden on the grounds that such entertainment was in honor of the gods. Gill states:

"This inherent idolatrous tendency was one reason for the suppression of these dramatic efforts."

The formation of church choirs and the practicing of hymns took the place of the old classical songs and dances, and a good deal of ancient lore of ethnological value was consequently forgotten.

* W. W. Gill, *From Darkness to Light in Polynesia,* pp. 252–253.
† *Op. cit.*

Arts and Crafts

Changes were also effected in the field of material culture. The scanty apparel suited to a tropical climate offended the missionary ideas of decency. The converts attempted to copy their teachers by substituting white bark cloth for the brown colored material hitherto worn, and later a demand for textile cloth was created. The missionaries carried a stock of cloth for their own needs and for trade purposes. The native women, on acquiring textiles, masked their beautiful figures in unsightly garments made on the pattern of nightshirts and termed "Mother Hubbards." The product of Western looms supplanted the native material, and the manufacture of bark cloth became a neglected and, ultimately, a forgotten craft. It is the irony of fate that, at the present time, civilized people in scantiness of attire have literally outstripped the natives.

A change in houses also took place. The white missionaries introduced a type of architecture that had been evolved in a temperate climate to keep out the cold. The native walls of upright stakes that allowed ventilation through the interstices were replaced by thick walls of wattled wood plastered with lime obtained from coral. The single-roomed house was supplanted by dwellings divided into many apartments adorned with Venetian blinds, but even the windows did not give such free ventilation as the native houses. When the tubercle bacillus was introduced by Europeans, the lime-walled houses retained the bacilli far more than did the open native houses.

The new types of houses were grouped on either side of a street in the neighborhood of a church. This entirely new arrangement was inaugurated by the missionaries in order that their converts could be near the church and the missionary school. The scattered inland house sites near the cultivations were deserted, and the population was grouped into villages for the first time.

The changes that occurred in the island of Mangaia are an example of what occurred in the various island groups throughout Polynesia. The missionaries, naturally enough, could not introduce their religion without carrying with it the foreign culture of which Christianity formed a part. Though traders and government officials have aided some of the changes, the most potent factor in the destruction of the old-time native culture was the death of the Polynesian gods.

Summary

The Christian missionaries introduced a religion that had been evolved in a different cultural setting. This religion carried with it its own cultural values, and the Polynesian values that centuries of practice had established in a different geographical setting were condemned as "heathen practices." The old taboos were replaced by new restrictions. The death of the Polynesian gods was followed by profound changes that, commencing with religion, extended to the disorganization of society and the wrecking of the native arts and crafts. The changes at first were tyrannical and but dimly understood. In the course of time, however, further adaptation took place, and the church and the government assumed their respective values in an adjusted culture. The Mangaians, as well as the rest of the Polynesians, have readjusted themselves to the Christian religion. If Christianity is any criterion of Western culture, the island communities of Polynesia are more civilized today than the masses in the great cities of Europe and America.

As an anthropologist, I see religion as an essential part of the culture of any people. Probably a psychologist or a theologian could phrase things better than I can, but I have attempted to avoid what has been termed "the verbal bondage of a sterile and paralyzing metaphysics." I have a firm conviction that the things man has created with his mind and worshiped in the spirit are as real to him as the material things he has made with his hands. A system of ethics may be sufficient for the intellectual minority, but it is devoid

of the feeling and emotion that appeals to the masses
of the people. The belief in the supernatural and in
the immortality of the soul must be accepted as real
facts that have led to action and results. I am not
concerned as to whether the supernatural and immortality can be proved or disproved scientifically. As
a student of the manners, customs, and thoughts of
peoples, I *am* concerned with their beliefs. The belief
in immortality is a living, vital fact that has brought
and still brings comfort and happiness to large masses
of people. But, though religion seems to be a necessary part of every culture, its value in Western civilization has been depreciating. Professor John Dewey,
in his Terry Lectures, held that the center of gravity
in our civilization had shifted more and more from
religion to economics. With many people money has
become not a means to an end but the end itself.

Our present civilization is sick and fast losing its
right to be called "civilization." The discoveries of
science, which should be utilized entirely for the benefit of man, are being prostituted for the wholesale
killing of people. The pity of it is that those nations
which desire peace are being forced to arm in a hitherto
unparalleled manner by those who desire to rule the
world by force. Truth has again sought cover in a
well from which she may never emerge. The Christian
ideals that religion has taught us seem to have been

cast aside by millions of people. Instead of brotherly love, we have racial intolerance and merciless persecution. Our civilization stands on the verge of a relapse, not into barbarism, but into sheer savagery. I believe that the Christian religion is an integral part of Western civilization or culture and that it is one of the few restraining forces that may yet guide us back to faith in goodness, truth, and justice. The death of the Christian gods would mean the collapse of the culture to which they belong just as surely as the death of the Polynesian gods led to the end of Polynesian culture.

Religion needs no scientific proof, for it is based on faith. Faith to those who have it is a vivid reality. Could we but restore that faith, we might be able to say to a sick world in the words of the Great Master, "Arise, go thy way; thy faith hath made thee whole."